Let's make tea out of roses

"Every branch in me that beareth not fruit he taketh away and every branch that beareth fruit he purgeth it, so that it may bring forth more fruit. "
St John: 15.2.

Dedicated to my loved ones –
My dearest family, my editor and friend Sharon, and David

Join me in a garden of prose and optimistic verse.
Poems to keep you company whether you are putting your feet up or wending your way through the wee small hours.
from "It is the heather candle that lights us, …. to
"If you clothed my mind with verse, Tea and marzipan cakes."

Book design by Sharon Andrews (Instagram @inksomnia_poetry/shandrews0913gmail.com)

ONE

A bee on a hurricane ride
Drums a tune of devilish pride
In her jet and yellow vest.

So quick to fly to honey combe,
So quick to find her way back home,
The April rain brushes past,
Her greedy jacket,
The sucking flowers, spilling,
Their sweetened magic.

No character could stop
The bee's manic path
Around the garden trees
Not even the hollyhock,
Wide and taut.

The whole garden Shook
When this pretty bee
Did her work,
Her black pedals buzzing through the earth.

Bee, bee come on, hit the breaks
For your little pollen legs, dangling,
Must need a rest.
The bee said
"I must catch the sun before it sets."
In her jet and yellow dress.

TWO

A miracle is not a mountain
Of gold,
Or losing the load.
It is not a green glade
Of milky shade,
Or half-lit hour
That made the grade.
It is not pride
An award,
It's the kind of thing
That hits you inside,
A whisp of trees on rolling hills
Collapsing into the skies.

THREE

Am I an autumn love?
Kicking leaves
Through thick ivy woods?

Or do I fit into every season?
Like each other crystalline person
In your warm glove?

I sing in spring,
She may skate in winter lakes,
I am listening

Am I an autumn love?
If so, I bow to summer
And squeeze tight winter's fingers,
And pay homage to may
And her returning.

If each fluttering leaf
Belonged to a trail
Would they reflect reasons
To be with you
every day,
in every vein,
Of every tiny leaf's frame
And all the seasons man may claim?

FOUR

Are you the *encyclopaedia Britannica?*
An odd kind of *hallelujah,*
A dark mourning for yesterday's scholar,
A nonchalant rhyme lighting up the sky.

If you are rivers circling the seas,
Little boats on thin, silver estuaries,
Or if you want to juggle with anemones,
Throw silent light on the ponds of
My memories;
Then, like a bird on the wing,
Gallop into the Night's harem
And mend the midnight prayer
Of History's lonely affair,
While rabbits in twilight grasses,
So lulled, whisker-thin
In ghost-like trances
Along the limp verse of humanity's lost chances,
Are dulled by the wet lids of time.

And tell me, how,
Close and candle-lit
We could not hear you
And do not hear you still.

FIVE

As the blue pebbles crush
Under the sea's voice,
I soar, I have no choice
But to circle the skies,
The blue moon that I lap.
You are there
On the other side of the tide.
I cannot give up the dampening stars
Where I abide
But I do want you.
Try to slip your cry
Into the still waters by.
Tell me you can fly
Above the dirty shingle
On the wings
You have been sleeping on.

SIX

Black thistle
Wet grass
Sing to me
Like a shy blackbird.
The brick yard
Spins my head
Against a willow
And a snow-white shed.
Caves, deep magenta
embalm the common parsons,
pagan chants.
Vast, blue, lake-green fields,
Old starry temples
Only charcoaled memories last,
The strawberry ties,
The barn geese,
Ditching the broken shell
Of rationale.
This wilderness,
It all makes sense:
Sad sunsets,
Wild amethyst-
All the grimy tragedy
Of a lonely, broken mind.

SEVEN

Blueberry shadows
Make rifts in the melodic dirt,
Episodic beauty.

Wind frets with the trees
And bends leaves,
Red rooves sunbathe
With smouldering lichen,
Sunlight in a light patter
Mottles the garden patio
Spectacular,
Episodic beauty.

EIGHT

Can I grab a chat?
Have a coffee in the garden centre
In the same way?
Can I visit home
And watch politics on television
Go to my room with the blue wall
And dine at the table with you for a meal
With a little wine?
Can I say things that don't make sense?
And plan my defence?
Will the days roll by in this mid-siesta?
The days of my life that are half way
Away from you and halfway running back.
Will the yellow daffodils
Glide in their sunny bonnets
In a garden of a thousand sonnets?
I do not want to miss you.
So let me tuck you away in my pocket
Where my childhood can stay,
Like a little locket
That I can open
On a rainy day.
A child's hourglass runs forever
But the sand in my hourglass
Shifts through different weather
So, can I grab a chat?
I do not want to miss you.

NINE

Come to the moon's grotto,
Lyrically,
Smothering the ellipse
Uncertainly,
The belly of ever widening scrutiny
A cove where slips the shore's
Ever beating rhyme
The stomach of grisly time,
Come to the moon's grotto
In the shallows
Of the nocturnal sea's silhouette
Where the rocks slash against the tide
With no scruples,
Only a hum
That a calling bird might hide.

TEN

Don't blush blue turtle
Resist your grudge
Ancient traveller,
Halt your waterwheel,
Just sail and gulp your violet prayers
Steering your homeward Vigil.
Swim *sea patriot*
Over the crying wave,
Without your sturdy oars,
Swim under the moon-moored stars.

ELEVEN

Don't be afraid of the *spinning wheel*
The rhapsodic notes of the earth's beat,
The drumming velvety crust,
Skin deep?

Be afraid of hurting yourself,
Disregarding accessible love,
Be afraid of skipping from your light,
From tripping.

Love all that is loveable,
Love the butterflies in your head,
The flowers growing from your arms,
Love the sweet parody
Of love's wrinkled step.

Hate the wrongness
Hate all the mess
Hate the missed chances,
Hate the opposite of bliss.

Don't be afraid of the *spinning wheel*
Be afraid only of skipping from your light.

TWELVE

Downward frail lashes, skirts around dream-loving eyes,
Blue eyes,
Your blue eyes save you.
It's in this sight, now, clearly, that I can see you are nearer
To me than before.
Parental re: fixing but not re: mixing
Would I swap you for that shifting sanctuary?
It's your blue eyes that save you,
Let that wild, crazy love have a pew
In full view of me, then you,
Because if we dream right,
If we soak up the earth's lustre,
If we let butterflies hang like butter
On blonde, misty, dancing leaves
Then I think you will stay,
It's your blue eyes that save you.

THIRTEEN

Flickering reflections like film stills
Cutting out around my mind,
Coming, going, refracting,
Sliding by, joined and re-entering
Make a lighthouse
A *window* to watch
Like Disney.
So, the sunlight ebbs
And the turquoise bluebells start to
Erase the day's fog and bristle,
There no longer seems a place for her gristle.
So floundering,
Perhaps a warm *hello* and
How does your grass grow?
The new windy shadow
Reason for the reticent flow and *I dunno.*
Perhaps a nod, smile will anchor me
To the evening smells
And chatter like bells may last me
To the later Night.

FOURTEEN

Her voice whispering
Through the night's bone,
Like a reed
Bent in its dying tongue
Asking her to drink
The salt of her sorrow
The salt of her prayers,
Dripping down the stairs of her soul.

FIFTEEN

Help is kind
Help is generous
Help is strong
Help steps along with us.
Help.

SIXTEEN

However, the light falls on the day
Be it chalky white
Or numbing grey
You will strike my nerves dumb
Rinse my bones of everything wrong
You will love me whatever the season,
Whatever words are buttoned in my lips,
Whatever hole may be in my reason
You will love me.
However, the night tumbles,
Whatever jumble my tears might stumble on.
You will repair
Every layer of despair
You will love me I swear.
You will love me
Every hour that topples into time
I know you can lift every sour grudge
That collapses my voice
Because your heart has known me
And for that I will rejoice.

SEVENTEEN

I am letting you go
With the broken snow,
The layers of trust and betrayal
Like mustard dirt on the snow trail.
I am letting you go
As the wind dusts the skies
I am letting you go
As the snow dies.
My laugh echoes back my tears
Because that was wilting petals,
Don't you know
I am letting go
And the snow may
Reverses her tracks
She trod so long ago
As she watches for the spring
When new flowers bud,
Watches, in the silken snow.

EIGHTEEN

I am on a spiritual drip
My crown is withering
Into the yellow earth
That I do not care to own,
Or leave tethered.
I yearn for the crest of sunlight
Bathing the restless tide
With roses' breath.
Drip, drip away
Rose of beauty
Drug like a smuggler,
Our heretic veins,
Running through us
Like rippling ravines,
Or woody vines of love.
Vermillion serpentine rose
Breathe life into our honeyed bones
Don't wait in the shadows,
The strangling gallows,
For they have flown
To absconding meadows.

NINETEEN

I am on this spit-roast
Round and round
My heart is shoved
Over the fires of hell's black glove
It is dark indeed
These days of slow release,
A breath taken
And then back spinning,
Back to the cauldron of an unquiet mind-
I did see angels on a hill,
The gulls that mended broken wings,
The man listening,
The woman trying
And lots of bright shiny things
That magpies collect sometimes in Spring.
As if my mind were sprained,
The dangerous thoughts
That made me lame
I did hear devils out in the rain
And will it ever be the same again?
But as the gravity of flame
Rises around my head
And love is not dead

And every mouth is open and absurd,
For what life,
What verse,
Can really reverse
The salty brain-wept tears
That I fear
Oh, so much do I fear.

TWENTY

I am startled in grass dew
By a sunset.
A traveller, I must set my limbs
On the starchy hills
Before opening my eyes
To the floundering meadows
Sweeping with frowns they wept.
My resolve I kept,
As I wished the fluffy dandelions well
On their flight,
The clouds and all the sunny shadows *fortune*
Monster trees *a drifting memory*,
A *saga* for their quick branches.
It was true I did not tell
Of that day
Of the daffodils that crept
In the seeded woods
I did not tell of the quiet load
I shed.

TWENTY-ONE

I buy you flowers once in a while
I cook you your favourite meal.
I clear the table often
I listen to jazz with you
I wine and dine you on your birthdays
I look at film leaflets in the afternoon
I do listen
You do talk.

You are a puzzle I must confess,
A confetti ball,
A ferocious tennis match
An arrangement to beat any orchestra
A movement, a scherzo.
And *Mrs Greenfingers* grows her flowers
And *Mr Film Star* plays his reels.

And down the ages
Of the lives of these two perfect pages
All I can do
Is sing your praises.
Happy Anniversary!

TWENTY-TWO

I don't think I can remember my mood.
I walked out of the door today and,
Caught in rambling tide of thoughts,
Mayhem,
And then, what was I thinking before?
What happened to my mood
A few seconds ago?
Sliding moods,
It's like dominoes,
Will they all come crashing down?
Rain, snow,
It's like a blurred lens.
Let them go.
A reel, a mural
I don't think I can remember ….
One mood brushing another,
Scratches of memory,
The photographs –
A pastiche of time.
I walked out of the door today
You know, I don't think I can remember my mood.

TWENTY-THREE

I have primroses in the blood,
Woods and trees slumber my breezy mind,
A hazel palette of green and columbine.
The pulse of life,
Like a scarlet knight is winning,
Let bells ring,
Let colour reappear,
Wait for the laughter round the corner,
A whispered encore.
Then days you cannot taste on the tongue,
Skinny, shot through with the ghost of evil.
But how impossible to tame the flame
That drinks the light,
Or bar the shadow that licks against her tight.
Perhaps only in sorrowful Night
Does our real sorrow meet her plight?

TWENTY-FOUR

I check my wooden barometer
On my wall in the corner
The reading is above mediocre
I think love is working today.

Sipping lemon under a tree
I watch a yellow canary
Out of her cage and free
I think love is working today.

Tugging at the goats
In the lazy yard
Lining the silver sky with a thousand clouds
I think love is working today.

The reading is above mediocre
From my wooden barometer
You caught a smile in the corner of my mouth
I think love is working today.

TWENTY-FIVE

If each step were a poem
How many would I have to write
To get to heaven.
My glassy bargains were so arduous
It's as if the mind were tripping
Dripping with sweat
From these years
Of climbing the turrets of self-worth
If each step were a poem
Am I there?
On that last stair
To mental health.

TWENTY-SIX

If you clothed my mind with verse,
Tea and marzipan cakes,
For better or for worse,
And if you sailed me down a river
With duckweed
And pink, dusted perch

If you put my mind
Under a sprig
Of lemongrass,
Put it by the door
With children's boots,
Rhymes and cuddles,
Till death do us part.

if you washed my mind
with sleep's tears,
if you pulled the hazel sun,
laughing, to my side,
love, honour and obey.

If you
If *you*
healed me.
From this day forward

TWENTY-SEVEN

In all shapes and forms
love comes upon us
like bright flags,
like a subtle glitter on a pavement
when the sun shines down
A chimney pouring out smoke
In a desolate area,
A lift over a gate,
A hand up out of a swamp,
A candle in a cottage
Love spreads its kaleidoscope
And hides flecks from us
Waiting for us to see the entire rainbow
An eternal adventure
It pushes and pulls,
Gently cajoles,
Demands and succumbs,
Plays with our minds
Why are the simplest things
Hardest to find?
And why do we drown so much beauty?

Are we still so frightened
To understand the majesty of love?
Crawling back to the truth,
Slowly and painstakingly
With fake mirrors all around us,
I'm sure that love
In its multicoloured splendour
Has only one message
Which is slowly clarifying, **trust.**

TWENTY-EIGHT

In time we will find our guardians
Who wait behind furtive doors
Like roses in mud huts.
Latent fear trickles through
Your cold hands,
Sinking swans
In our darkest dreams
Where the devil makes war
Out of liquorice canons.
A backward glance
At the dull officers we were,
The romantic fools.
So, calm our torn medals, *Apprentice*
And build the fires of life
In amongst falling nettles,
The parasites
And the wilting petals,
And find us remotely
In between thistle and buttercup,
Yellow lawns of indolence
And innocence.

TWENTY-NINE

Is there always a listener?
There is always a listener.
Is there always love?
There is always love.

Do you always stay in misery?
You do not stay in misery.
For we dare to love,
And pity loneliness
For there is always a listener
Is there always a listener?

THIRTY

It is not the routine,
The OCD,
The habitual back and forth.
It is not the paper that keeps catching light
As the little flame picks its way
Along its flight.
It is not the swarm,
The crowd pleasing
Drone
That waxes and wanes
The whole day through,
It's the few,
The solitary bee,
With her little spear of honesty,
Soaked in her pastel path of piety
That speaks to me.

THIRTY-ONE

It is now that the sky is blue,
That the moon sits in her round shield,
Now that the grass shares time with the fields.

Too long have I left the day to herself,
The hours to lengthen their grim shadow
It is *now* that each second must grow.

Only *now* do the crops lay their harvest on us,
Does the bird catch the morning light.
It is *now* we are the most bright.

Can *NOW* be loved in all her gentleness
Render her spirit to us?
It is by her dishonest promise
That *now* is the only thing we miss.

THIRTY-TWO

It is the blanched candle,
The silhouette,
Slipping across the sky like an ivory sickle
That stole our hearts away.
As she ploughed the Night
Her crop of snowdrop stars,
Mute,
Her curves
Like a bright clasp swerve.
Memories blurred to us,
Bright moon rolling like scrolls
Of winter leaves,
Slow down your tide,
Night dreamer.
Can I glimpse your beautiful ball?
Until midnight
When I will yawn the yellow day
And forget the magician that once came my way.

THIRTY-THREE

It seems the scrambling
Of time's gracious sliding rule
Is like the blink of a ghostly schedule,
Mammoth and small.

Furtive this war never halts
Or slackens,
Never sheds her hopeless wings
Of peeling bracken,
Where the gentle blowing
Of linoleum
Meets the cold day.

Too cracked to shove away
The restless hour
Too sad to lay her head
And pray,
The little clock
Waits patiently.

Brimming with love's foray
And woken,
She translates
The new lineage
That has been spoken.

Time can only tread
On this agate,
Her wild and shy ransom
Shaking May's buds
Until all trees submit
To this pulse,
Tall as pines,
Strange as pouting goldfish
And old as the first step
She ever took
On earth's mists.

THIRTY-FOUR

Lightening flares
Her nutmeg frames,
Captions in the midnight air
Staring like a startled camera
And scared.

Obscured by thunder
Like a skeleton
She remembers the yellow dusty roads,
Green felt crickets,
Innocence,
And summers of sweltering rose.

Bright thickets
Overtook her measled breath,
Her bruises,

And her ladder to the sky
Flashed in front of her eye
Like a bonny memory
of the dusty yellow roads.

Holding onto the ghost of strife
she passed through the tight knuckle of Night,
loving the bony rose of life
even though the high and low
gave her vertigo.

Round and round the maypole
The bones met their match
For all around the darkness
The yellow dusty road still flashed.

THIRTY-FIVE

Like a drunk leopard
Watchful of the smells
Of the night
A voice unfastens
Fang-teeth
Ghosts of death
From her panting loins,
Yellow blood-eyes
Telling us this bodkin
Of terror has fled,
Can be no more.

THIRTY-SIX

Love, honour and obey.....
This one is to keep......
Love, honour and obey.....
This one is to sleep with....
Ripples secretly keeping watch over me.
Life's troubles,
My sprightly *campion,*
There, a *lamp,* by the wayside,
Lighting the shadowy puddles,
Sturdy and resilient,
This friend is to cherish.
Hardly a blemish on love's
Walnut skin

This is the day when fun walked in,
When your smile followed mine
To the school canteen,
A sister, bubbly like a chatty stream,
Breathing giggles into our cardigan sleeves,
A female constabulary,
Up to our knees,
Laughing through the trees,
Mouths full of strawberries'
Straw hair in straw barns,
Like locks falling from our arms,
Our memories
Are like wire telegraph cables,
You are logged.
Message sent.

THIRTY-SEVEN

Love whistles amongst the trees
Outstretched and full of seeds
For longing
Love has a way, In its sway
Of grouping us
Like a little orchard.
We like, plump apples,
Cider-makers
And lonely fruit
Can only belong to the tree,
Until the sky dries the bark
In glorious sunshine
And we are lit
Like hundreds of marbled sparks
By love's whistling seeds
And arched breeze
Amongst the trees.

THIRTY-EIGHT

Gossamer soothes the hot dry earth
Gently cradling its agitated stems.
It clothes, wraps and delicately soothes
The steaming sod.
Misty, hazy, white as silk dust,
Drifting lazily, sifting through broken leaves,
Brittle twigs and melted daisies,
Petals strewn upon the sizzling ground....
.....
Pecking the gold dust
Two cooing woodpigeons
Remove grit from the dusty powder of morning.
Broken breadcrumbs
Lose the daisies and their sweet content
Shove them into corners of restless uncertainty.......

THIRTY-NINE

My ever- changing mind
Weaves like a dappled golden loom
Bright and untangled.
Glorious thoughts
Rise and fall like little spirals
Calling.
My head floats
As if I am sitting in silver ships,
As if the marine sky
Was puffed with dandelion stars.

Soaked in stars like little jars
Spilling through time
Like swimming diamonds
Now my mind rhymes.
I find the mottled nerve,
Again,
The opened cage
Of every season of reasoning.

FORTY

My love is snug like the swollen rain,
Back to you and back again
Along the track of heather's vein,
A lattice of journeymen,
A crossroad of chance,
Whistled romance,
For I try again.
This layered soul,
Droll,
Soft as earth
Melds the willow,
Bird's twigs
Of the thrush
Into the heat, the light,
Until a blush
And back again to you
Who is who?
Or are we all in one blood-rose
Of exotic smell,
The plaided crossroads
Between heaven and hell?

FORTY-ONE

My soul looks at you through a cracked window,
The autumn leaves lie bare in still woods,
The little bench that I stamped my secrets on,
The air, the feel of midnight blossom,
The magic softens
When I think of you.
The sea draws back our love
And throws it carelessly back to its kiln
Of passing.
So, our loss is shaken
And it hurts like buckled waves bleeding...
But I count each wave every day
Until the Night's moon
No longer lights the spray
And my soul looks at you
Through a dimming window.

FORTY-TWO

Picking up my broken mind,
A delicate lotus blossoming,
Scrolling through the fractured light,
I can find gems of might
Nerves that slip like lemons
Through my gullet,
Nerves that soften like pollen needles,
Settle like cotton flowers
Nerves like razors,
Nerves, *my nerves.*
Oh, what paradise
My thoughts are pencil-straight,
Linear once more,
Floating back to shore,
Those nerves giggling in my throat.

FORTY-THREE

Running a million metres
Around the milky way
Won't you *stay*?
Here with the green figments of trees,
Hollowed out nests
Of bumble bees,
Won't you *stay* with
The fish foaming in the seas,
The telegraph poles
Dialling out memories
To captain's wives,
Stay with crippled leaves,
Dying estuaries,
Stay with ill-at-ease fretful folk,
Biting lips,
Ghostly fingers
Shaking at hope.
Won't you *stay*?
It really is a field of poppies here
And we do love to have you near,
A magenta illusion
Decanting the veils of fear
To the doorstep of queer time
And let's, yes, leave it there.

FORTY-FOUR

Sealed,
It is this yelp from the heart,
Every time it starts
I just know it is *this straight away sound*
From my heart that punches the world
Fair and square,
Not the lonely sound of considered replies,
Well intended lies.
So now, bang, what I want to say is
Let's love our way to Hollywood's
Dizzy lights and calypso Nights.
Who dares wins, hey it's not an easy world,
But flimsy selves survive the wells of woe,
The whispered shells of suffering.

FORTY-FIVE

She held a heather candle
Lighting the handle of darkness
In grim madness
Putting away her guard and pretence.
Resting her sleepful hands
On the soft landing
Gently weighing her slow spirit
Against the night's fray
She walks the plank of her dreams,
Quiet screams trickling away like streams,
Mauve flowers dressing the wounds
Of tomorrow.

FORTY-SIX

No one to say you're talking rubbish
No one to say you're weak
No one to patronise you
No one to give you the abuse you seek.

No one to say, well you do have a point
No one to say you will grow up one day
No one to say you're just a speck of sand
No one to tell you the way.

No one to say try listening
No one to say there's plenty like you
No one to say it's a terrible world
No one to say you haven't got a clue.

No one to say you don't exist
No one to say heaven's the answer
No one to say *keep smiling*
No one to say you need chemical enhancers.

No one to say some people have to take drugs
No one to say it's like a diabetic
No one to say we can't all have strong character
No one to say your argument is pathetic.

No one to say *go slowly*
No one to say patience is a virtue
No one to say it's sweet being quiet
No one to tell you what to do.

Someone to tell me I am special
Someone to tell me I am all right
Someone to tell me I'm different
Someone to tell me I'm me.

FORTY-SEVEN

Tattered prayers I bequeath thee
Along the walls of naked sacrifice,
The battlements of strife.
Your hearts, dolphin-blue
Linger their smoke signals,
Genies in the sky.
For what Titanic
Rolled the tongues of cyclops
The eye of tongues?
We, mermaids of salvation
Hear the sea's granite roar,
The stones lifted
And washed away
With shredded joy,
The sad beat of mercy turned,
Fish disappearing in yellow shudders,
Thin and churned.
What ghastly Titanic
Picked us up by the hook,
Shook us, beat us
And threw us away?

FORTY-EIGHT

Tell me a tipsy verse
To make the day less blue,
A sparrow on the wing
A cherry blossom's hue.

Hear the wobble of my pen,
The window catches my eye
A tree nodding in time
With the warm breeze's breath.

How quickly the sun goes down
The ink rounds up my words,
Sad but true.
The bird's brief song
Won't still be here
When the night has begun.

FORTY-NINE

The bird perched on the tree
Head, at once, with orange beak, cocked
His eyes looking at me,
And singing relentlessly.

My thoughts,
A rocking horse of reminiscing,
Betrayed my mood
And there the daring bird stood.

How I stared
At his little throbbing heart,
His slick feathers of deep blue,
Dark as the bark.

Then I sung fervently,
Into my lungs
And out into the woods,
And for an instant I was He.

Struck by this doppelganger,
I could only kiss the boughs and leave,
His ghost reaching after me.
And he opened his wing
To say farewell,
Not to me, but to the trees.

FIFTY

I saw him
Yesterday
Quietly
He sat
In a bank of dandelion
White petals blowing
Like feather clocks
Against a submarine sky.

Below
Fish swam like accordions
In the clink of
Tambourine streams
Under the arch of trees,
Wet cuffs on windmills.

Yesterday I saw him
He sat
Quietly
A chime of fish
Still swimming under
The spiralling trees,

His face lost in the time
And colour of the sky.

FIFTY-ONE

The dusk of *straightforward*
Is in plain view,
The dangled tomorrow,
A clear avenue,
Cuffed with poplar trees,
The rails of sleepy stairs
Show me the way
To sure-footed days,
Ribboned,
Taste liquid on the tongue,
Madagascar mint,
Sea-blue,
A fairground of possibilities.
Love exists in my realm,
Dare the darker shades of hell away
From burnt angels.
Love carries with her *proposals*
Which one of us will open the letter?

FIFTY-TWO

The ointment of this earth
Keeps us quietly from unquiet rehearsals
In dim-lit churches.
In whispers we do say
I laughed wrong,
The corners of my mouth creased backwards,
My tears fell awkwardly,
My jagged scars ill-fitted me,
I fell upside down and I crawled the wrong way round.
And the Earth says;
Bathe in the river of God,
For each ripple Is like a silken, treasured call,
The voice of echoed, crying souls
And these words, *this mouth did not crease,*
And I did not crawl the wrong way round to you
This time.

FIFTY-THREE

The sun flaps in the wind
As she scribbles her voice
On the fragments of cloth-trailing trees
Borrowed from a poet.
Does she owe him a quote?
The afternoon rolls on and predicts
The petals' colour
And the return of evening song
Let there be no Light that does not freckle
No dusky leaf that glows not in Her waterfall,
Lemon blue, that does not offer her lease
To the Night.
Again, loving the round dusty sun,
A poet in the morning
And as the day is done.

FIFTY-FOUR

The white night
Too grey to be old
Screams her wizened ashes
At the cold.
Her hands getting colder.
Embellished like a tentacled crucifix,
But stony and rigid
Do not rise,
But rise
As the day wakens
And the Night closes her crusted eyes
Limp in the equinox,
Being pardoned.
Dark rise
With your emblems
Like leopards,
Lotus petals around
Your figurehead
And do not anymore be dead.

FIFTY-FIVE

There is a hush in the trees,
A restive feeling of contented leaves
Shuffling in the midnight forest.

No leaf could be poised so evenly
No leaf so enigmatic in its beauty,
No leaf crumpled
In such array could prepare the woody floor,

Laden with bluebells
Softly making a misty
Hood of azure,
Like jewels.

We are plucked from the leaves,
The diamond trees,
In the turquoise breeze,
Lulled by the black,
Flightless Night.

Perhaps the forest's light,
Indigo in colour
Is enough to welcome
The new day and the new night
Through the hush in the trees,
Shuffling in the wooded leaves.

FIFTY-SIX

Threads of blushed sanity,
Breaths,
Are flickering through my eardrums, my thoughts, lucidly.
Like cream from fattened cows,
Hearing clearly
Vowels like vows from chapels
Pealing
For long-forgotten messiahs
Deep in the birch,
Their benchmarks sat for us to remember.
Thoughtfully
I breathe streams of glugging breath,
Falling onto my shoulders,
Wrapping round my knees.
I breathe I breathe.
It's everything to breathe like this,
Battleships can sink around my wrists if I can breathe.

The mind in its coffin of wax cannot turn back,
Refract.
We are milestones within signposts that, with dread,
Look ahead.
Conkers hitting conkers,
Forests overlapping trees,
Even they breathe.

The sun wobbling autumn sunlight
On the mauve heath
Can we loosen our need to breathe
Into every chink of shadow,
Light every lamp post along the way?

Each step meets the next,
Autumn minds climb just one more step,
And hay forks tiptoe on harvests
Vast with cotton corn
And we are reaping, reaping,
Gleaning the intellect,
Reckoning, laughing in haylofts.

FIFTY-SEVEN

Through the marshlands
She held her own gravity,
Bossing the stars
To leave their levity
And sink into the aprons
Of her melancholy.
She held her own gravity
Longing for the moon
To wade with her,
For the night to kiss her gently,
And ever so evenly
To tread, like a moth
Over her body
With the authority of two beady eyes
Reckoning her.

FIFTY-EIGHT

To suffer this half mad mind of mine
To slip brokenly between
Black, mauve, grey,
To stand inside summer hay
And blackened winter days,
A hay loft over a stable
And a putrid river under the stream
My love recaptures
Is a life's moral foraging,
The sunset's final delving
Into the sand that keeps
Our toes glowing.
It is knowing that we can leap
Between love and death
And Her showing,
We can find what Hercules was towing
And blessed hearts keep rowing
Through those battled waters
Keep rowing, rowing.

FIFTY-NINE

Walking a little cobbled and tired,
Sweating for home,
I passed the ragged waft of
Dog rose
The petals casual,
The light ample,
The path ordinary
The mood way up there.

A memory pale as the blue-pink petals
Washed over me those few seconds
The scent reached my nose,
And all of a sudden
The road was aglow with rose.

SIXTY

We are coal-purple grapes
With a stake in the earth's crust,
Bobbing and toppling over each other
We have romances with dust.
But how often do we remember
That brave little seed
That planted us here,
Our life to bear.

SIXTY-ONE

We call this not a sin,
Not a calling from a learned man,
Not a verse to understand,
Not a step that was wisely planned.
We call this "crime",
Hurting from each side of the land,
We call ourselves beautiful
With outstretched hands,
We writhe in innocence
And we, like delicately flaming instruments
Claim from the scythes of Spirit
Misunderstood relics,
Hissing in dried grass
Where snakes curl and die gently in the dark.

SIXTY-TWO

When that last climb
Over the rickety style
Was taken
I was awoken
From a trial
The grass was springy
Underfoot
Tears lingering,
Shed silently.
Looking back
To the stretch of styles
Like a tramline of hurdles,
It is miles
That we scaled.
We are heroes
In our own dreams,
Saints,
Of a battle we relinquished
For our saviour's sins.

SIXTY-THREE

With this ring I thee …
Miscarriage of my heart…
Will you stay?
My blossoms are worn
I am stained
Is love's cup?
With this ring I …
Settle to the music of a Yew
Split like a walnut shell,
Sin's broken wages…
With this ring I thee wed…
Fickle, Faithful, Fanciful
Signed.

SIXTY-FOUR

You are a dream screaming
A heap of prayers listening
You wake me
And you still me
You are a solitary ride
But don't be.

I can't make you out
You live with the bees
And it seems
In my head?
Traversing deserts
Jumping brooks
You are one step ahead.

You are clouds circling clouds,
Bendy trees
Every sparkle on every wave
And you are light.

Give me your flute
Your Nightingale's shrill note
Give me your bloody sinew,
Your sweating eyes
Give me your galloping heart
And above all this, your damned love.

SIXTY-FIVE

Your story is earth-bound
Soliloquy,
What chalk on what blackboard
Whistled hymns,
Wrote the psalm
That spoke in rhyme,
What prophesy
Of what proportion,
Split my mind,
What song
Is yet to make history?
Lost in your narrative
I meet myself again.
You are ashes and the furnace
That shapes our fate,
a blistering anvil that rises in the east
and sets, indigo, at the pearly gates.

Printed in Great Britain
by Amazon

85469496R00045